Melancholia

I can suck melancholy
out of a song as a weasel sucks eggs.
More, I prithee, more.

JAQUES *in Shakespeare's*
AS YOU LIKE IT

Melan

cholia

by Adam Horvath

with illustrations

by Valeria Zecchini

 BABEL EDITIONS

FIRST EDITION, SECOND PRINTING.

Poems copyrighted by Adam Horvath, 2021.

Cover, *Solitude (Melancholia)* by Giorgio de Chirico (1912).

ISBN: 978-1-956200-00-3

For Julie

Love of my life, my best friend,
and my first and best reader.
These are all for you.

And for Tim, Greg, and Sara

Watching you grow has filled me with joy.

Impartiality of the Door

Don't just stand out there.
Come on in!
Or turn around and leave now,
if you prefer.
It's really all the same to the door.

Contents

Melancholians Grapple with the Inscrutable

Interlude

Into Deepest, Darkest Melancholia

Adieu to Melancholia

Welcome to
Melancholia!

⇝ ⇜

That strange flower, the sun,
Is just what you say.
Have it your way.

The world is ugly,
And the people are sad.

WALLACE STEVENS,
Gubbinal

Rainbow

Imagine, if you can —
and I really do hope this requires some effort —
a dystopia called Melancholia
where the world is ugly
and the people are sad.
In Melancholia,
sighting a rainbow causes no one's heart to leap up.
Just the opposite.
Lovers, seeing a rainbow, are cast into despondency,
stop holding hands,
and trod on glumly,
avoiding one another's glances.
Those lucky enough not to be in love
are convinced it's an ill omen.
The cynics among them are convinced
leprechauns have cunningly contrived
to place booby-traps at the rainbow's ends,
and that the rainbow itself
is merely there to lure the unwary.

Morning in the Anthropocene

After showering in ionically-enhanced Alaskan rain water
    (Aqua-Volta™)
and wolfing down a bowl of organic phytonutrients
    (Phyto-Noot™)
with camel milk imported from the Gobi Desert
    (Cam-Moo™),
while seated on my Happy Fingers™ massage chair
beneath a Sol-Brite™ sun lamp
I used the EZ-Zazen™ app on my Smartee-Pants™ mobile phone
to meditate for 30 seconds
upon the meaninglessness of existence
and the utter futility of all action
before dashing off to work.

Cloudburst

The sky split open and rain poured down in sheets.
The gods weeping at our folly?
Or just divine micturition?

Oxymoronic Onomastics

They named it "Happy Valley"
because all the residents were despondent.

Trouble in Paradise

The glower.

The furrowed brow.

The Soprano in the Bullpen

Let's face it.
I'm not going to get my ducks all lined up in a row
before I've bought the farm.
And I doubt my ship will come in
in time for me to save my fat from the fire.
They say there's a silver lining in every cloud.
Perhaps. But I can tell you this much,
it never rains but it pours.
I know, I know,
it ain't over until the fat lady sings.
But correct me if I am wrong,
isn't that a soprano warming up in the bullpen?

Life in the Past

I've always wondered what it must have been like
to be alive in the past,
when everything happened in sepiatone,
and a mere blush on the cheek
would have sparked a riot.

Memento Mori

Memo to Self: Someday, and not so very long from now,
like the Malagasay hippopotamus,
the Lesser Mescarene flying fox,
the Eastern Canary Islands chiffchaff,
Newton's parakeet,
the Aldabra brush-warbler,
the Cape Verde giant skink,
the Ascension flightless crake,
the Passenger Pigeon,
and of course the Dodo,
you, too, will be extinct.

Mixed Message

The house reeked
of bonhomie
when you first walked in.
But by and by,
you could detect
a fragrant whiff of
misanthropy.

Eye of the Beholder

A monster,
to another monster,
must be a thing of surpassing beauty.

The Covert Agent

He's a very cagey misanthrope,
always beaming
and extending a willing hand.

Homespun Anthropomorphism

Pointing up at
the thick blanket of clouds,
my wife announced,
hopefully,
"Look, dear, the Sun
is trying to come out."

"That's very nice,"
I replied.
"Please ask him
to try a bit harder."

The Indictment

Convinced I had behaved unbecomingly toward her
in her dream last night,
she confronted me about it when she awoke this morning.
Brushing aside my protestations of innocence,
she judged me insufficiently remorseful
and declined to speak to me all day.

The Forecast

Scattered glimmers of hope early today
will give way by mid-morning to doubts and uncertainties
as problematic and morally ambiguous situations
sweep down from the north and move across our region.
By this afternoon, irksome vicissitudes will prevail.
Expect gusts of existential angst, guilt, and remorse,
possibly severe at times.
Tonight, there will be occasional lamentations
followed by fitful sleep.

The Beneficiaries

Starlings and grackles shall inherit the skies.

Jellyfish shall inherit the seas.

The cockroach lurks
beneath the floorboard,
biding its time,
grinning.

Common Fates of Familiar Things

The book you are holding right now
(if you are reading this in a book)
may have been pristine when you first picked it up
but it will soon enough
smudge
or stain
or tear
or become dog-eared
(if it hasn't already).
You will wince at the first blemish
and chide yourself
for being so careless
or clumsy,
and resolve not to let it happen again.
But of course, it will.
And you'll probably esteem the book itself,
as an object,
just a tiny bit less for its newly acquired defect.
But the fate of your new book
merely foreshadows the individual fates
awaiting all the familiar things around you,
without exception.
And it is probably for that reason that you chafed

when the original blemish occurred.

So contemplate the eventual fate of all those familiar things,
the things whose very familiarity confers a feeling of comfort
that can't last.

Sooner or later,

they will all

craze

crack

smash

shatter

wrinkle

fade

tatter

fray

shred

unravel

crumble

degrade

dissolve

droop

wilt

ossify

rust

erode

decay

tarnish

28

corrode

mildew

grow moldy

rot

putrefy

stink

tilt

totter

tumble

collapse

implode or explode

be smashed to smithereens

ebb

wane

founder

sink

dwindle

shrivel

dry up

turn to dust

blow away

dim

grow fuzzy

fizzle out

or disappear entirely

and be lost to memory,

which is itself
already slowly loosening its grip
on things that were once
(*so recently!*)
still graspable,
seemingly unforgettable.

Hope (There is No)

There are many hopes in a lifetime,
but there is no Hope.

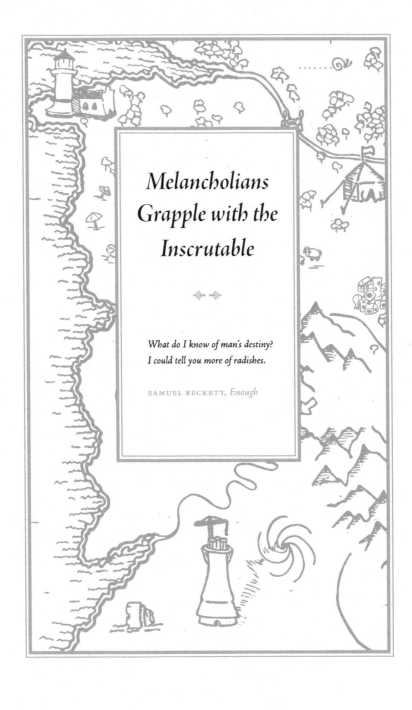

Melancholians Grapple with the Inscrutable

❧ ⚜ ❧

What do I know of man's destiny?
I could tell you more of radishes.

SAMUEL BECKETT, *Enough*

How Irony Got Its Start

Here's life! *L'chaim!*

It's great, ain't it?
Now go out and have yourself a ball.
Take a stroll around the garden
and think up some nice names
for all the animals.

Oh, by the way,
I almost forgot to mention,
you'll die later.

What?????
Why are you looking at me like that?

Just Sayin'

No one ever asked *me*
if I wanted to be part of your fancy new "Creation".

Just sayin'!

And while it was nice of you to think of creating a "helpmeet" for me,
was it really necessary to rip out one of my ribs to do that?

Just sayin'!

And whose idea was it
to plant that low-life serpent in the garden
to sweet-talk an impressionable young woman
into nibbling your precious "forbidden fruit"?
(Isn't that called entrapment?)

Just sayin'!

And wasn't it a bit extreme
to impose the death penalty on us
and all our descendants
for what was essentially a misdemeanor?

34

Feeling Misunderstood

"You don't understand me at all!"
God complained.
"You have no idea what it's been like for me
all these eons.
I thought, when I allowed hominids to evolve,
I would get some respect and appreciation.
But frankly, it's been nothing but grief so far.
Wars, idolatry, petty larceny, you name it.
Why did I even bother?
It's been just one headache after another.
Homo sapiens sapiens?
Ha! That's a rich one!
Things started to go downhill
sometime after I stirred up the primordial soup.
Plants seemed like a pretty good idea at the time.
But animals were, let's just say,
problematic,
even *before* I let the hominids evolve.
Remember the dinosaurs?
Those were a flop!
And as far as people go
it's been pretty much a mess ever since "Adam and Eve"
— I'm speaking figuratively, of course —

you *do* know those are made-up people, don't you?
Bedtime stories for credulous hominids
dreamed up by other hominids
just to amuse themselves.
All that stuff about the serpent and the so-called apple
is just a lot of *hee-haw*.
Don't believe everything you read!
But as I was saying,
I really don't think you understand me at all.
And if you think *you* have it tough,
just try being Omniscient and Omnipotent
for a while.
Maybe for an eternity."

The Foreknowledge Conundrum

When you've attained full geezerdom,
you might find yourself tempted to lament,
"If only I had known back then
what I know now."
But not so fast.
If you'd known *then* what you know *now*,
surely you would have made plenty of different choices,
leading to different outcomes.
Isn't that the whole point?
So, when you got to be your present age,
you could never know
the things you know now
that you wish you had known back then.
Put that in your pipe and smoke it.

The Solipsists' Club

Following a lecture he had just given,
the philosopher Bertrand Russell was approached
by a woman who professed to be a solipsist,
and said she was "surprised there aren't more of us".

The monthly meeting of the Solipsists' Club
will take place on Tuesday evening at 7:00 PM.
I *imagine* you will all attend.
And as *you* may well *imagine,*
I will be there too.
It will be a pleasure to see all of you there.
The topic for that evening will be:
"Coping with Loneliness".
I, myself, wouldn't dream of missing it!

The Skeptic's Skeptic

The Skeptic:

"I don't believe
we will ever fathom
the true nature of things."

The Skeptic's Skeptic:

"I doubt that's so."

Jean-Paul Sartre in Purgatory

Haunted by the spectres of dead philosophers
whose clamorous debates over questions like
"Does existence precede essence?
Or is it the other way around?"
and "Why is there anything, and not just nothing?"
and "Does the moon cease to exist when I look away?"
reverberate in his memory,
Jean-Paul Sartre spends his fitful posthumous days and nights
at his favorite sidewalk *café* on the *Boul' Mich'.*
The coterie of doting admirers
who once hung upon his every utterance
as if he were a living god
has vanished,
leaving Sartre sitting all alone,
chain-smoking,
hovering over a *demi-tasse* of espresso,
restlessly toggling between
the *plaisirs* of Being
and the *longueurs* of Nothingness.
Pen poised in mid-air,
he stares at an empty notebook
and finds himself unable to summon a single witty *mot*
or provocative *pensée* worth jotting

on the blank page that returns his stare
tauntingly.
Just now a troubling thought takes root in him:
"Should I have been kinder to Simone?
Probably so.
But I suppose it's too late for that now, isn't it?"

Descartes Flirts with Existentialism

René Descartes brandishes his quill
and dips it into an inkpot.
(The *machine à écrire* hasn't been invented yet.)
A droplet of ink dangles from the tip of the quill.
Descartes stares out the window
and hesitates before writing.
"Which sounds better? 'I *think*, therefore I am'
or 'I *am*, therefore I think'?
That last one has a nice ring to it!
But is it too Existentialist for the 17th century?"

Dream Fragment

At first,
I thought it was some exotic,
man-size,
fern-like plant
unfurling itself
in the rain forest.
But as I drew closer
I saw it was actually
a cowled figure —
a monk, perhaps? —
making his way painstakingly
through a churchyard garden
overrun with ferns,
moss and lichen-covered rocks,
and weatherworn tombstones
bearing barely legible names and dates.
Like the tombstones,
he seemed ancient.
I knew somehow that he was on his way
to make his last confession.
I could tell,
the way you just *know* things
in dreams.

He was weary,
and he craved absolution,
longing to hear the words
"Pax vobiscum"
or
"Go and sin no more"
that would let him finally rest in peace.
When I awoke at dawn,
I prayed he might be granted
the release he so fervently sought.

The Conduit

She crouches by the fire.
Her hair is disheveled
and she has a wild look in her eye.
As if in a trance,
she starts uttering her poem aloud
exactly as it is occuring to her.
The young man at her side listens intently
and copies it, word for word,
onto a scrap of weathered parchment.
The poem is about fire and ice.
A howling storm.
Strange creatures flying through the air.
Time and Eternity.
It distills wisdom drawn from
an unknown wellspring.
She plunges on
even if some of the language
spilling from her
is unfamiliar.
"A singular concatenation of events unlikely to recur."
She repeats that verbatim.
When the words finally stop coming,
she sighs deeply.

Her body slackens
with a shiver.
The two companions exchange looks of quiet amazement.
The poem lingers in the air between them.
She is shyly proud,
and a bit frightened
by what just took place.
But this isn't the first time it has happened.

Cul de Sac

"The only way 'round
is through,"
Robert Frost sagely observed.
What he neglected to mention is
there's no way out.

Thirteen Ways of Responding to the Human Predicament

The raised eyebrow
The look askance
The shrug
The headshake
The muttered imprecation
The grimace
The wan smile
The mordant chortle
The fit of hysterical laughter
The fist pumped defiantly in the air
The sigh
The compulsive yawn
An irresistible urge
to curl into a ball
and sleep.

Interlude

❦ ❧

*Only beings can dream of
the impossibility of non-being.*

EUGENE THACKER,
Infinite Resignation

Chuang-tzu Thinks About ...
Nothing

Chuang-tzu awakes with a puzzled look,
a furrowed brow,
gazes around the room,
sees it is filled (hardly surprisingly) with little bits of *everything*,
you know,
all the usual stuff —
lamps
chairs
bedroom slippers
dustbunnies
yesterday's newspaper
a slice of leftover pizza
the urn containing his father's ashes –
all manner of odds & ends.
But a single thought courses through his brain.
A question actually.
Why is there something, not nothing?
Can there even *be* anything called "nothing"?
If so, just think about all the things *not* in it:
skyscrapers
juice blenders

argyle socks
the Himalayas
poems like this one —
why, the list is endless.
There'd be no end of nothing.
But really nothing endless, either.
"It's a conundrum, for sure," Chuang-tzu thinks,
"a real head-thumper.
Yes, I must give it some more thought.
But first, what's for breakfast?"

Chuang-tzu ("Master Chuang") was a Chinese sage whose life straddled the fourth and third centuries BC. An influential exponent of the Taoism associated with Lao-tse, he is admired for his subtlety and sophistication, and is often considered a "proto-Zen" writer because of his skepticism, whimsicality, and love of paradox. He is probably best remembered for his "Butterfly Dream": "Now I do not know whether I was then a man dreaming I was a butterfly, or whether I am now a butterfly, dreaming I am a man."

Brunch at the Absurdist Cafe

What's the *marsupial du jour* today?

Ah yes, opossum bisque,

let's start with that.

Chocolate babka? Bring it on!

Lizard gizzards? No, none today.

But the flamingo *flambé*

with a *nouveau riche* sauce

sounds divine.

And a platter of petite mixed emotions

drizzled with *trompe l'oeil* will go nicely with that.

A bottle of the 1954 *Haut Bourgeoisie* will be just the ticket.

And for dessert? The *escargot gateau* is certainly tempting.

But could you top that off with

just a dollop of *Weltschmerz* please?

That would be so decadent!

Cause for Alarm?

Should I have been alarmed?
Or merely amused,
when I arrived home a bit earlier than usual
last evening
and caught my philodendron
perched in front of the TV,
watching a re-run of
Little Shop of Horrors?

Playing It Safe

They claim it'll cross the Atlantic in under a week!
I doubt it,
but even if it's true,
I'm not setting foot on the *Titanic.*
Nosirree, Bob!
I'm staying put right here
in the house I just built
on this slope of
Krakatoa.

Long-Winded

He was notorious for his
long-winded quips,
tedious puns,
and seemingly interminable
aphorisms.

Dining al Fresco

Let's meet for pizza
at Chichen Itza.

Later, spaghetti
in the Serengeti.

Calamari fritti
in Tahiti?

Bouillabaisse
on the shore of Loch Ness!

And in Campeche,
dulce de leche.

Less

Some say too much is never enough.
Others maintain that less is better than more.
If *they* are right,
and less *is* better than more,
then I suppose
more of less
must be far superior
to *less* of less
and less of more
preferable to
just plain more.
More or less.

The Orca in the Bed

"It's like having an orca in the bed!"
my wife declared
as I tossed and turned
struggling to find a comfortable position.
I didn't bother to reply,
but with a meaningful flick of my tailfin
as I dove beneath the covers,
I flung a gentle splash of saltwater
in her direction.

Chuang-tzu Feels the Weight of the World

It was peach blossom time
and Chuang-tzu knew he ought to be composing poems
in praise of the silvery moon
as the peach blossom petals slipped from their branches
and floated down the stream
like haiku written on scraps of paper.

Instead, he had spent the entire morning
watching the news on television,
which he knew was a very bad decision,
and eating Cocoa-puffs straight from the box
with a soup spoon,
which he knew was *another very bad decision*.
But he just couldn't help himself.

Now, he felt the weight of the world upon him.
He kept asking himself,
why so much *tsuris* and *mishegas*
on our poor little planet?

56

Chuang-tzu inverted the nearly empty cereal box and gave it a good shake.
The last handful of Cocoa-puffs tumbled out onto the table top.
He arranged them into half a dozen little hexagrams,
or at least what looked like they *might* be hexagrams.
An ad hoc Cocoa-puff *I-Ching!*
Chuang-tzu peered at the Cocoa-puffs, trying to discern a pattern
—some kind of message that would mitigate
all of that *tsuris* and *mishegas*.

What have we got here?
It looks like water, mountain, wind, mutability, abyss, and thirst.
He squinted and peered at the hexagrams again.
They had wiggled around a bit.
Now they looked like fire, meadow, thunder, shadow, obedience, and mirth.
Chuang-tzu was sure there must be some hidden significance there.
But try as he would, he couldn't make heads or tails of it.
He sank into gloom.
If only he hadn't eaten so many Cocoa-puffs!

There was only one thing to be done.
After all, it *was* peach blossom time.
"I shall write a haiku in praise of the silvery moon," Chuang-tzu resolved,
"and set it free to float down the stream.
Perhaps someone will find it and read it
and find some relief from the world's misery.
Or perhaps not."

Into Deepest, Darkest Melancholia

❧ ❦

"Would you tell me, please, which way I ought to go from here?"

"That depends a good deal on where you want to get to."

"I don't much care where."

"Then it doesn't matter which way you go."

LEWIS CARROLL
Alice in Wonderland

Report from the Piltdown Men

Deep in a cave beneath Barkham Manor in Sussex
where they've carved out a cozy nook for themselves
amidst the stalagmites and the stalactites
(the ones that point up and the ones that point down,
in case you've forgotten)
a group of Piltdown Men
(not to be confused with the rock & roll band from the 1960s
who went by that name —
the ones who gave us that unforgettable tune
"Brontosaurus Stomp",
which you can still listen to on their 1998 CD compilation album
The Piltdown Men Ride Again)
— no, not *those* Piltdown Men,
but the authentic ones
(don't believe everything you were taught in school!)
the ones who are the so-called "missing link".
(They really *hate* being called that, by the way,
although they're more or less okay with "*Homo piltdownensis*".)
These Piltdown Men
with their human-like craniums and ape-like jawbones
have fashioned a state-of-the-art laboratory
deep below Sussex,
where,

clad in safety-goggles and white lab coats,
and having already demonstrated to their own satisfaction
the flatness of the earth
and the heritability of acquired traits,
they are now busily at work,
utilizing water painstakingly distilled from dripping stalactites,
and report they are now just days away
— perhaps only minutes away! —
from achieving Cold Fusion.

The Last Cricket

Summer ended weeks ago,
so I wonder what keeps *you* in these parts.
I do notice your chirps are getting a bit slower
and further apart.
Do you want to know how I imagine you?
Like the last Roman Centurion
garrisoned in Britannia,
far from home,
charged with overseeing foot traffic
along a slowly degrading segment of the road
that was once one of the glories of Rome's imperial reach,
not so very long ago.
The rest of your garrison must have either died off,
gone back home,
or gone native and intermarried,
leaving you alone behind
to deal with the locals,
Angles and Saxons mainly,
who stare back uncomprehendingly
as you chirp *"Quo vadis?"*
and when you get no response,
simply *"Vale."*

Time Travel

If I had a time travel machine
I would take it for a spin
and drop into Ancient Athens.
I'd know I had landed at the right place and time
if I saw a sign like this at the outskirts:

NOW ENTERING
ANCIENT ATHENS
POP. 136,219
431 BC

I would hang around the *Agora* for a while,
eat some *dolmas,*
chat up the locals,
listen to the authentic philosophers philosophize

while avoiding those pesky Sophists,
who were always lurking around
waiting to pounce on any rubes
who'd cough up a few *drachmas* to hear them.
I might catch a tragedy or two over at the Dionysus Theatre.
The hottest show in town back then was *Medea*.
A bit of a downer!
But hey, it's a tragedy,
so it's *supposed* to be.
(But I've heard the chorus is fantastic!)
Tickets are as scarce as hen's teeth,
but maybe I'd get lucky.
Before climbing back into my time machine
and heading home,
I'd build a miniature golf course
right around the corner from the Parthenon
where there'll be lots of foot traffic.
Yes, a fancy miniature golf course
with little sand traps
and windmills
and hidden tunnels.
Just to prove I had actually visited
from the future!

On the Merits of Living
in Upper Slobbovia

Upper and Lower Slobbovia made their first appearance in Al
Capp's classic hillbilly comic strip *Li'l Abner* on April 4, 1946.
They were conceived as a large iceberg, whose hapless residents
were perpetually waist-deep in snow. The favorite dish of the
Lower Slobbovians was raw polar bear (and vice versa). Upper
Slobbovia, for its part, was the native habitat of the Schmea-
gles, birds who flew so fast they could not be seen.

There's one good thing you can say about living in
      Upper Slobbovia.
It sure beats living in Lower Slobbovia!

Life in the Slobbovias (Upper and Lower)

Let's just say it's not exactly paradise on earth.
The two Slobbovias, Upper and Lower, occupy a large iceberg
roughly the size of Freedonia,
or the Duchy of Grand Fenwick,
whose hapless inhabitants live waist-deep in snow all year round.
Icicles dangle from their noses.
The 14th edition of the *Michelin Guide to Upper and Lower Slobbovia*
informs us that raw polar bear meat is
the Slobbovians' favored *plat du jour*.
And as for the polar bears,
their culinary taste, unsurprisingly,
runs to raw Slobbovians.
A very nice symbiosis is at work there!
The relationship between Upper and Lower
(or as it's sometimes called, *Lowest*) Slobbovia is complicated.
As the bottom surface of the iceberg is gradually hollowed out,
seawater rushes in,
and the iceberg grows topheavy.
Periodically,
it flips right over,
so what had originally been Lower (or Lowest) Slobbovia

and Upper Slobbovia

trade places.

(I told you it was complicated!

Try not to think too hard about it.)

The important thing to know is that Upper Slobbovia

is the exclusive habitat of the Schmeagles:

birds that fly so fast they can't be seen!

To quote the *Michelin Guide to Upper and Lower Slobbovia,*

"Intrepid travelers

who venture to the Slobbovian region

will find the arduousness of their journey amply rewarded

by a visit to the fabled Nesting Ground of the Schmeagles."

Runaway Train

Wherever I travel,
things quickly unravel.
That patch of scenery gliding silently past the window
is just a blur
tinted a wan, watery hue by the glass.
I know what I see out there
is not what it seems.
With a lurch,
the train springs to life
like a creature possessed,
gathering momentum,
slowly at first,
then ratcheting it up,
faster and faster,
until at last
it's blazing along the rails,
rocketa-rocketa,
at breakneck speed.
Depopulated towns
and empty platforms
whiz by at a giddy clip.
Leaving the towns behind,
we hurtle across farmland,

where I can make out misshapen beasts
skulking in the fields.
Some mill around
with their backs to the wind,
staring off into the distance
sullenly and uncomprehendingly.
Others wander out under a glaring sun
onto a parched landscape
stubbled with tree stumps
and tiny, desiccated shrubs.
The sun plummets.
Night swoops down
and swallows the train
in a single gulp,
plunging me into blackness
and confusion.
An eerie stillness has settled over everything,
as if we are hovering in mid-air.
But where exactly are we?
I think I remember having departed, once,
from a station, somewhere.
It seems so long ago now!
And that station's name
has long since slipped from my memory.
But will there ever be a destination?
And where are all the other passengers?

70

Adieu to Melancholia

❧ ❧

"Is it life?" he answered, "I would rather be without it," he said, "for there is queer small utility in it. You cannot eat it or drink it or smoke it in your pipe, it does not keep the rain out and it is a poor arm-ful in the dark if you strip it and take it to bed with you after a night of porter when you are shivering with the red passion. It is a great mistake and a thing better done without, like bed-jars and foreign bacon."

FLANN O'BRIEN, *The Third Policeman*

Chuang-tzu Tumbles into a Recursive Vortex

Chuang-tzu has a dream in which he is sound asleep
dreaming that he is sound asleep dreaming
and in the dream in the dream in the dream
he wakes up and strides across the room
to gaze into a mirror
in which another mirror (on the wall behind him)
is reflected
so that he sees a reflection of himself
reflected
and re-reflected
not exactly infinitely, but seemingly so,
until the receding Chuang-tzus become *really tiny*
— minuscule homunculi —
and Chuang-tzu dreams that his thoughts about this,
which aren't terribly profound, to tell the truth,
— something along the lines of *"Gee whiz!"* —
appear in a little bubble over his head
— a cartoonish bubble,
like the ones invented by Rudolph Kirns,
who first used balloons to express dialogue
in his *Katzenjammer Kids* around 1900

— thought bubbles that are now, of course,
replicated over and over
in all the mirrors of Chuang-tzu's dream of a dream of a dream,
as Chuang-tzu himself is.
When he finally awakens
from his dream of dreaming of dreaming
the very first words that pop into Chang-tzu's head are,
in fact,
"Gee whiz!"

Warp Speed,
the Snail's Way

Upon sighting his beloved
at the far end of the twig,
the snail puckered up,
lunged forward,
and hurled himself toward her
precipitously,
at a pace of one mile per year. *

* roughly 7 inches an hour

Warp Speed,
the Zen Monk's Way

Upon being informed that a certain tree
blooms only once in a century,
the *sensei* commanded
"Then we must plant one immediately!
We haven't a moment to lose."

No Attachment

When I assert
there's no ego attachment to the things I've written,
I am referring to my alter ego,
of course.

The Booklover's Lament

Books will be written
long after I am dead.
Someone else will read them.

In the Twilight Zone

As the sun sank,
the sky gazed down at the mountains and lakes below
and sighed,
thinking to herself,
"How crepuscular I feel right now!"

Moon Struts its Stuff

Ah Moon.
I know that glow!
I've seen it before.
I bet you're getting ready to boogie tonight.
Am I right?

This Way to the Egress

with a nod to P. T. Barnum

Here's your hat, what's your hurry?
And please don't slam the door as you go out.

The Impact

A poem,
if thrown at a pane of glass,
should shatter the glass.

DANIIL KHARMS

Thanks so much for coming today.
I hope you enjoyed that last poem in particular.
It packed quite a wallop, didn't it?
I bet you didn't see that coming!
Please watch out for the shards on the floor
as you exit.

Bashō Discovers Nietzsche's Doctrine of Eternal Recurrence Avant la Lettre

Same damned pond

Same damned frog

Same damned *"Plop!"*

(Sigh)

Adam Horvath

Adam Horvath grew up in Bayside, Queens, and studied English at Columbia, where he was infected by Chaucerian irony and the "metaphysical ideas and scholastical quiddities" of John Donne & Co.. He never recovered. After a two-year stint as Navigator of the cargo vessel USS *Arcturus*, he embarked on a career as a senior acquisitions editor at several university presses and a trade book editor for McGraw-Hill. His translation of Alejandro Casona's play *Suicide Prohibited in Springtime* was published in *Modern Spanish Theatre* (E.P. Dutton) and was performed on the Canadian Broadcasting Corporation's radio network. He once memorably had breakfast with the great Argentine fabulist Jorge Luis Borges. His desert island reading list includes *Don Quixote, Archy and Mehitabel,* and everything by Thomas Bernhard.

A devout polysemist who also relishes the occasional pun, Adam now lives in Oregon's Willamette Valley with his wife, Julie, and a pack of very frisky pet peeves. He is preparing three new collections of his poems, *Flamingo Heaven & Other Lofty Concerns, Chuang-tzu Rides Again,* and *Invasion of the Clerihews.*

Melancholia by Adam Horvath

is the first Babel Edition, published under the direction of Griffin Gonzales after a first printing from No Reply Press. The project was begun in 2019 after the discovery by Mr. Horvath of a realm called MELANCHOLIA, which he documented thoroughly over the following year. Cartographer Valeria Zecchini was dispatched to Melancholia to map its terrain. During her sojourn, she also sketched some of the region's denizens. Her depictions are printed alongside Mr. Horvath's poems.

Made in the USA
Columbia, SC
26 August 2021

43928646R00049